AF270896

YOU'RE THE LOAF OF MY LIFE

Thunder Bay
P·R·E·S·S

San Diego, California

Thunder Bay Press
An imprint of Printers Row Publishing Group
10350 Barnes Canyon Road, Suite 100
San Diego, CA 92121
www.thunderbaybooks.com
mail@thunderbaybooks.com

Printers Row Publishing Group is a division of Readerlink Distribution Services, LLC. Thunder Bay Press is a registered trademark of Readerlink Distribution Services, LLC.

Correspondence regarding the content of this book should be sent to Thunder Bay Press, Editorial Department, at the above address. Author or illustration inquiries should be sent to Summersdale Publishers Ltd, 46 West Street, Chichester, West Sussex, PO19 1RP, United Kingdom, www.summersdale.com

Publisher: Peter Norton • Associate Publisher: Ana Parker
Senior Developmental Editor: April Graham Farr
Editor: Stephanie Romero Gamboa
Production Team: Jonathan Lopes, Rusty von Dyl, Beno Chan

ISBN: 978-1-64517-462-2

Printed in China

24 23 22 21 20   1 2 3 4 5

TO..

FROM....................................

I LOVE YOU
A LATTE

You make my
heart skip a

BEET

WE'RE OTTER-LY
ADORABLE TOGETHER

YOU
DONUT
EVEN KNOW HOW
MUCH YOU MEAN TO ME

YOU'RE MY TWEET-HEART

You're my

BUTTER HALF

YOU GOT A
PIZZA MY HEART

YOU BET
GIRAFFE
I LOVE YOU

YOU
BAKE
ME CRAZY

I love you
more than I can
BEAR

YOU LIGHT UP
MY LIFE

LET'S
AVO-CUDDLE

TOGETHER
WE'RE
MER-MAZING

There's so

MUSHROOM
in my heart
for you

TOGETHER WE'RE
DINO-MITE!

I'M NUTS

ABOUT YOU

ALL I WANNA
DO IS
TACO
'BOUT YOU

You're top
KOAL-ITY

YOU'RE
CHERRi-FFiC!

WE HAVE GREAT
CHEMISTRY

I

FIND YOU
RIBBIT-ING

It takes two to
MANGO

HEY,
GOUDA
LOOKIN'

YOU'RE REALLY
SO-FISH-TICATED

YOU HAVE MY
SEAL OF APPROVAL

I love you to my
CORE

LOVE IS A GAME
TOUCAN PLAY

YOU'RE
PIE-FECT

YOU'RE
WAFFLE-Y
CUTE

I love you
BERRY
much

WE MAKE SUCH A
GREAT PEAR

I'VE
FALLEN
FOR YOU

YOU'RE MY
SOY MATE

You
make me
HAP-PEA

FRANKS
FOR BEING
MINE

I'M DEVOTED
TURTLE-Y
TO YOU

YOU'RE ONE IN A MELON

You're a complete
HOT-TEA

YOU MAKE
ME FEEL

SAUCY

WADDLE

I DO
WITHOUT
YOU?

LETTUCE
CELEBRATE
OUR LOVE

Let's never SPLIT

YOU MELT

MY HEART

YOU'RE
GOURD-GEOUS

OUR
LOVE IS
MEOW-GICAL

If I've
GOAT you,
what else do I need?

I THINK YOU'RE
EGG-CELLENT

YOU'RE A
FINE-APPLE

YOU GIVE ME
PORPOISE

We were
MINT
to be

YOU'RE MY
BOO

I LOVE YOU
FROM MY HEAD
TO-MA-TOES

YOU MAKE MY
PROBLEMS SEEM

IRR-ELEPHANT

ALOE you
VERA much

i WON'T GO
BACON
YOUR HEART

I'M A HOPELESS
RAMEN-TIC

THANKS
FOR PUDDIN'
UP WITH ME

I WHALE
always love you

REMEMBER
SOME-BUNNY
LOVES YOU

YOU'RE THE
LOAF
OF MY LIFE

If you're interested in finding out more about our books, find us on Facebook at THUNDER BAY PRESS and follow us on Twitter at @THUNDERBAYPRESS.

www.THUNDERBAYBOOKS.com

IMAGE CREDITS

YOU'RE
PIE-FECT

YOU'RE ONE
IN A MELON

YOU BAKE
ME CRAZY

YOU'RE A
FINE-APPLE

LOVE IS A GAME
TOUCAN PLAY

TOGETHER WE'RE
DINO-MITE!

You make my heart skip a
BEET

I WHALE
always love you